Look out for a
FREE MAS
Inside this Annual!

You Will Need:

- Thin elastic, wool or string

- Scissors

- Sticky Tape

Instructions:

1. Pull out the perforated mask page.
2. Pop out the mask.
3. Cut enough elastic/wool/string to fit around the back of your head.
4. Attach to the back of the mask with some sticky tape.
5. Have fun with your new mask!

SCISSORS ARE SHARP! ASK AN ADULT FOR HELP BEFORE USING.

Welcome

Welcome to the wonderful world of Olly Murs! Dive in for loads of facts and fun

Pedigree®

Published 2013.

Pedigree Books Limited, Beech Hill House,
Walnut Gardens, Exeter, Devon EX4 4DH

www.pedigreebooks.com | books@pedigreegroup.co.uk

The Pedigree trademark, email and website addresses, are the sole and exclusive properties of Pedigree Group Limited, used under licence in this publication.

The Smash Hits® trademark is the sole and exclusive property of Bauer Consumer Media Limited, used under licence in this publication.

Content and format: this Smash Hits Annual 'Special' is published as an independent tribute, with all included material sourced and openly available in the market for use, and is not published in conjunction with Olly Murs or their management

All images courtesy of Rex Features

ISBN 9781907602900

Olly

Olly

Fantastic facts

Mad about Murs? Here's all the top facts you need to know about the man himself!

Full name Oliver Stanley Murs

Date of birth 14th May, 1984

Star sign: Taurus

Born Essex

School days Went to Notley High School, Essex

Siblings A twin brother called Ben and a sister called Fay

First discovered On the sixth series of The X Factor, when he came second after being pipped to the post by Joe McElderry

X Factor audition song Stevie Wonder's Superstition

Fave football team Manchester United

Before he was famous Olly was a recruitment consultant

Fave singer Michael Jackson

Fave song Billie Jean by Michael Jackson

Fave music video
Bruno Mars – The Lazy Song

First single ever bought Friday
Night by 911

Fave clothing brands Farah,
Fred Perry

Fave colour Blue

Fave female singer Lana Del Ray

Most shameful artist on his iPod
Jedward

Top holiday destination Barbados

Fave Muppet Animal

Fave foods Bananas, cheesecake
and ice-cream

Dislikes Tomatoes and negative
people

Superpower he wishes he had
X-Ray vision

Celeb crushes Cheryl Cole
and Mila Kunis

Olly

Olly

An X-cellent adventure

He went from a boring office job to the top of the charts. Olly's been on quite a journey to get there

Olly Stanley Murs was born in 1984, Essex to proud parents, Peter and Vicky-Lynn. Growing up, the cheeky chap was a keen footballer and in his teens played semi-professionally for Witham Town. Sadly, he had to put his dreams of being the next David Beckham on hold when he damaged a ligament in his knee, and instead he put all of his energies into music, forming a covers band with his friend Jon Goodey called Small Town Blaggers.

With a football career out of the question, he focused on becoming a professional singer. And in 2007, while working as a recruitment consultant, he decided to try out for The X Factor. Sadly he didn't quite make the cut, but unperturbed he tried his luck again the following year...

After another knockback he decided to take some time out. So he threw some clothes in a bag, hopped on a plane and went backpacking around Australia. It was while he was there that he decided that it could be third time lucky, and when he arrived back in the UK, he decided to give The X Factor auditions one last try.

Olly auditioned for The X Factor three times!

He wowed the judges with his rendition of Stevie Wonder's Superstition, prompting Simon Cowell to say it was "the easiest 'yes' I've ever given". He went on to make it through Bootcamp to Judges' Houses, and before you could say 'tight trousers' he was on stage at the live finals, praying that the audience would like him as much as the judges did.

His first live performance of Robbie Williams' She's The One, won him a legion of fans, and week after week he was voted through to the next round. When the final rolled around, Olly lost out to Joe McElderry, but he came a respectable second and was soon snapped up by Epic Records and Syco Music.

He swiftly began work on his debut self-titled album and released his first single, the Number One hit, Please Don't Let Me Go, in August 2010. He embarked on a theatre tour in April 2011, and later the same year he supported the mighty JLS on their arena tour.

He released his second album, In Case You Didn't Know, in November 2011, and his third, Right Place Right Time, followed in November 2012.

Cheer up, Olly — you've had three hit albums!

Meanwhile, Olly's TV career took off when he was asked to co-present The Xtra Factor alongside Caroline Flack in both 2011 and 2012. He also dipped his toe into the modeling world, becoming the face of clothing store NewYorker, as well as showcasing designs from Robbie Williams' clothing label Farrell.

As for the future? Olly has revealed that he plans to concentrate on his music — even if it means that his TV presenting has to take a back seat for a while. In the words of the man himself: "In 10 years time, I'll be close to 40, so I hope to be in a position where I'm financially stable and I've got a great family and friends behind me. Hopefully married, hopefully kids, that I'm enjoying singing and that people still like me. If I'm still doing tours, still performing at this level, then I'd be delighted."

Olly plans to concentrate on his music career

Essex boy

Thanks to **TOWIE** everyone is talking about Essex, and there's no doubting Ollie loves his home county!

On nights out

"I prefer going out with my mates in Essex, where I can do what I like, have a good time and don't have to worry."

On the support from his Essex natives

"I'm proud of being from Essex, and proud of the support I've got. I hope I can continue to make them proud with my music."

On Essex guys

"I think you know we all have that kind of swagger. I'm a bit more cheeky than arrogant, I think some Essex boys can be a little bit too arrogant... My mates are like that, but with me I am a little bit more cheekier and I don't really take myself too seriously."

On being away from his Essex home

"It's always tough being away from friends and family. I'm very much a home-boy."

On being recognised back home

"I just get on with it. But in Witham I just walk up the street and I've got family and friends around me, and everyone has a laugh with me and we all get on really well. No one really bothers me that much really."

On TOWIE

"I've never watched TOWIE. If you live in Essex you tend to hate it because it's not really a true representation of who we are."

Olly

Olly

Discography

Singles

You Are Not Alone
(with the X Factor finalists) 2009

Please Don't Let Me Go 2010

Thinking Of Me 2010

Heart On My Sleeve 2011

Busy 2011

Heart Skips A Beat
(feat Rizzle Kicks) 2011

Heart On My Sleeve 2011

Dance With Me Tonight 2011

Oh My Goodness 2012

Troublemaker (feat Flo Rida) 2012

Army Of Two 2013

Albums

Olly Murs 2010

In Case You Didn't Know 2011

Right Place Right Time 2012

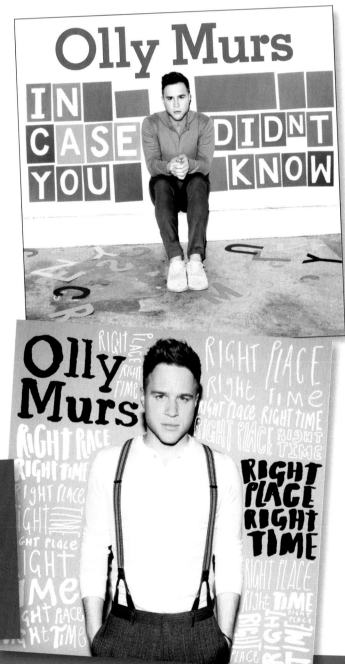

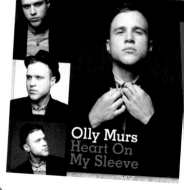

Live!

Olly is never happier than when he's on stage singing his heart out

Clever Olly matches his suit to his set

No Olly, the audience is not an orchestra...

Guess what number my last album went to?

Olly sings a lovely ode to his hat

Olly performs on a giant silver wedding cake

How many flop singles have I had?

25

Olly

Olly

Funny faces

Olly Murs is a man of many faces. Some of them silly

Olly was very excited about the giant picture frame

Olly does his best pout. At least we think it's pouting...

Come on Olly, surely the banners aren't that rude?

Olly was delighted when he won the gurning competition

Did you know?

⭐ Olly has been nominated for four BRIT awards to date, but has yet to win one. Boo!

⭐ Before he became a solo artist Olly was a member of a covers band called Small Town Blaggers.

Olly Murs or Matt Damon? You decide!

⭐ He tried out for X Factor twice before finding success in 2007.

⭐ He once went backpacking around Australia, and it was while he was there that he decided to give The X Factor another go.

⭐ Olly once turned on the Christmas lights in Cribbs Causeway, South Gloucestershire and a whopping 7000 fans turned up to see him!

⭐ Thanks to his good looks the singer and presenter has been mistaken for Hollywood superstar Matt Damon in the past.

⭐ He's a keen runner and goes sprinting every other day.

You can't pull the wool over Olly's eyes!

⭐ The cheeky lad appeared on Deal Or No Deal back in 2007, but he only won a tenner. He also appeared on a celeb version in 2012, making him the only person ever to appear on the show twice.

⭐ A fan once wrapped themselves in wrapping paper and turned up on his doorstep!

⭐ His third album Right Place, Right Time was the fastest-selling album of 2012 by a male solo artist. Impressive!

⭐ Olly's nan is his number one fan and knits wooly hats for him!

⭐ He listens to cool old-school crooner Otis Redding when he's feeling down.

⭐ Olly wishes he had written The Beatles classic Yesterday, because he could "Probably live off the royalties for the rest of my life!"

⭐ Olly had a small role playing himself in American drama 90210. Fancy.

Olly

Olly

Say what?

There's no doubting Olly is a cheeky chappy — check out these cute quotes!

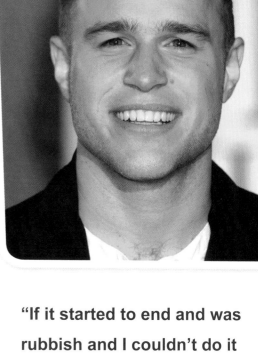

"Whenever you're in a relationship, you have that favourite song that reminds you of when you first got together or when you first kissed and then every time you hear that song, it reminds you of that person."

"I wanted to write a song for my fans. That's what Army Of Two is meant to mean — it's about me and them, although it can be about any relationship."

"I genuinely love giving presents to my family. I didn't used to have much money for Christmas presents, but this year I will definitely be spoiling them rotten!"

"I'm a bit of a perfectionist. I'll watch myself back on Xtra Factor and want to do it again because of a few hiccups."

"If it started to end and was rubbish and I couldn't do it any more, I'd be annoyed. I love what I do and I'll continue to do this for the rest of my life."

"I'm a workaholic. I love working. I hear people say I'm the hardest-working man in the pop industry at the moment. I've always been like that. I've got a great work ethic."

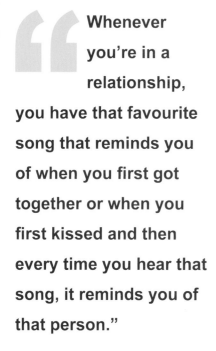

"I'm not really a troublemaker, more of a cheekymaker."

"I'm an entertainer and a performer, and I admire the likes of Justin Timberlake, Michael Bublé, Robbie Williams. They're all solo artists who can hold a crowd in the palm of their hands."

"If people want me here, then people will continue to buy my records. And if they don't, well I'm quite happy to go back to Essex and live a normal life. That's not a problem."

"I get involved in everything I do musically. It's an important part of what I do, and it's something I'm very proud of. I want the music to feel like it's my music, typical of my personality."

"What One Direction have done is absolutely streets ahead of what any other British act has done in the States. It's a

"I'll never stop performing. I wanna still be doing this in 10 years time."

phenomenon that's very rarely replicated — once in lifetime stuff. Britney, Beyoncé, Justin Bieber, Rihanna..."

"You never know what a woman is thinking, so don't ever try and second guess her or figure out what she's going to do. Just please her in any way possible and make her happy. And then she'll be happy!"

"You can have all the talent in the world, but if you don't work hard at it, it'll never come to you."

"I can play guitar – but not to a high standard, and I'm learning to play the piano after my tour as I've just bought a grand piano for my house."

"Yeah, I think I have changed. I don't think it's for the worse, but I think when life changes around you so drastically, your way of living changes, too."

"I think when you find a job that you love and when you're good at something, it just makes you more confident.

Yes, I am pretty fabulous!

Why we love Olly

Why do we adore Olly? Oh, so many reasons...

He can style out a slip up!

Olly has fallen over on stage more than once, most recently on his 2013 tour. And every time he gets up, dusts himself down and carries on like a true pro while everyone lols along.

He does a lot for charity

The kind chap trekked through Kenya in 2011 in aid of Comic Relief alongside other celebs including Lorraine Kelly and Dermot O'Leary. He was struck down by a stomach bug towards the end of the grueling walk, but he still carried on like a trouper.

He's a sensitive soul

Talking about online bullying he admitted, "For all the hundreds of thousands of tweets you get that are lovely and amazing, unfortunately you will always notice the one that's horrible. I think every artist that says they don't see it or get affected by it is lying. If you look at it, it is going to affect you in some shape or form."

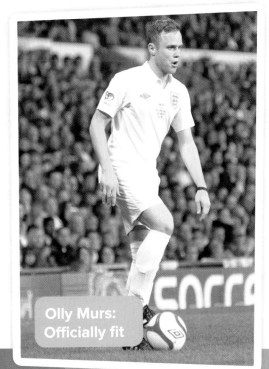

Olly Murs: Officially fit

He strips off!

Olly promised to strip naked if his debut single 'Please Don't Let Me Go' went to number one. It did and he bared all in Heat magazine. He's certainly not shy!

He's fit! (In more ways than one)

As well as doing loads of running and playing football, Olly has got himself a personal trainer to whip him into shape. He says, "I'm probably the fittest I've been in a year or two. I don't think I'm as fit as I was in 2010 – I was in good shape then! But now I'm getting there, slowly but surely."

A date with him would be fun!

Olly's already got his next date all planned out – and says he would date a fan if she was the right girl! "Well obviously it would be a nice lady and just really traditional. Pick her up take her to a nice restaurant, go to watch a really, really good film... then see her for a second date. Then hopefully on the second date have a bit of dinner at mine or hers, have a bit of Wii action or maybe go bowling or something active."

Olly

Olly

Style king

Mr Murs is one of the best dressed pop stars on the planet. We found out his style secrets

It's no secret that Olly is a big fan of hats and he says the one thing he can't do without is his trusty trilby. "When I'm touring and I'm on stage my hair gets all sweaty and horrible so there's no point in me trying to keep it nice. I can't live without it!"

He also admires other people who wear hats. Who are his hat heroes? "Jacko, without a doubt! Just for the one that he wore for Billie Jean, really. But I love some of Jamiroquai's big Indian-looking ones. They were awesome."

Hats off to Olly – he nails good headgear

JK likes to go for the understated look

He admires Jacko's choice of trilby

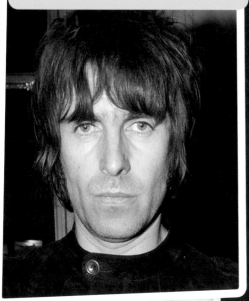

Paul Weller and Liam Gallagher are two of Olly's top style icons

Mr Murs knows how to work a sharp suit

As for his style icons, he keeps it old-school with some fellow singers. "I like Paul Weller, Liam Gallagher, the mod look, that whole era of music. Preston of The Ordinary Boys as well. I think he's always put a lot of effort into his outfits. He's always been cool."

Olly says splashing out on togs is something he's loved doing for years. "I always go out and buy clothes, that's probably my luxury, my guilty pleasure, to be honest. I am always out buying clothes."

He's also good at doing research before he hits up the shops so he knows what he's after. "There's nothing wrong with spending an extra hour on the internet just trying to think of your outfit, so that when you go shopping you're a bit more prepared."

His style has changed over the years and he's happier with the way he dresses now. "I think you change with the times. Being on TV and in photo shoots, I'm involved in music and fashion a lot more than I used to be, so my style has definitely changed – for the better, of course."

Now he knows what looks good on him, don't expect him to mix things up too much! "Now, I've pretty much found my style and I won't change for the next 10, 15, or, 40 years. I've found what I love most about clothes, what works for me and what suits me."

What are his style tips? "For me, it's always colour. You've always got to have the right blend of colour. You'd be silly to match a yellow T-shirt with a light green pair of

Yep, we give a thumbs up to this look too

trousers, you know?"

He also advises mixing up high street with vintage and designer brands. "I mix and match a lot: sometimes I'll buy from boutiques, sometimes I'll buy vintage clothes, sometimes I buy big, expensive labels, but 70 per cent of the time, my clothes are from the

high street. I always buy TopMan jeans, but I shop everywhere."

He also recommends being yourself when it comes to fashion. "Wear what you feel comfortable in, because people will like you for who you are rather than trying to be someone that you're not."

43

Olly

Olly

Papped!

Wherever Olly goes the paparazzi go too!

Not that he seems to mind too much...

Olly loves talking on his invisble phone

"I could've sworn I put it in my pocket"

We hope he's put an iron on his birthday list

Olly did well in the speed-walking championships

"Look, that man's taking my photo!"

A few of his favourite

Just some of the things
Olly thinks are a-Murs-ing

Michael Jackson

The legendary Jacko is Olly's favourite pop star of all time and he had been a fan since he was young. He even sang a version of his hit Can You Feel It when he appeared on The X Factor.

The Goonies

The vintage '80s movie makes Olly laugh and he's tweeted about his love for it several times. If you haven't seen it, check it out!

Skittles

The sweets are Olly's favourites and he often gets given them by fans, the lucky guy.

Singing

Not surprisingly singing is Olly's favourite thing to do. He says if he had to choose between performing and presenting, he would choose singing every time. Good to hear!

The 'Olly Wiggle'

Ol's fans created the nickname the 'Olly Wiggle' in tribute to the way he shakes his hips back in the early days, and he thinks it's 'hilarious'.

48

things...

David Beckham

Beck is Olly's fave footballer of all
time and he says of the talented
chap, "Beckham was my idol,
I wanted to look like him, I wanted
to play like him, I wanted to have
a girlfriend like his."

Tea

Olly loves a good cup of tea and
incredibly he holds the Guinness
world record for making the most
cups of tea in an hour!

Manchester United

Olly was introduced to Man U
by his dad, who is also a big fan.
He reveals: "I'm a massive United
fan, I've been supporting them
for a long time now. I've got a box
there and a season ticket, and
I've supported them ever since
I was a little kid."

Hats

You'll rarely see Olly without a hat, but
he reckons his collection is starting
to get a bit out of control now...

95-106 CAPITAL FM

THE UK'S NO.1 HIT MUSIC STATION

HELP A CAPITAL CHILD

Olly

Olly

Tweet tweet

Olly's a bit Twitter fan. Here's are some of our faves so far. #lol

"Got proper sore feet today!! Not sure why, Not sure how!! But they are. NIKE Pumps are on!!"

"I was like Sir Steve Redgrave on the rowing machine at the gym this morning..."

I've decided that my dad @MRFUZZYMUZZY73 is never going to watch UNITED live again.. That's 3 games, 3 defeats when you go!! Never Again!!"

"Had my 1st cheat meal in a few days... Cheese & Marmite toastie at airport!! #mouthwateringgood"

"Just watching Dinner Date.. These lads can cook.. I'm such a terrible cook.. this lady would get Beans on toast from me with Cheese.. Haha"

"Mr Horan @NiallOfficial loving the new chest hair dude.. #niallsgrowingaloverug"

"I've literally been a sleep the last 24hrs... That was needed.. Including the McDonalds & lots of Homeland season 2!! Lol"

"Getting a football in the thighs outside playing 5a side proper hurts! Aint felt this in a while! Right inside leg #RPRTTour2013 in Cardiff!"

"insane.. I've met someone that has a bigger Jaw than me haha #hugebobblehead"

"Doing some circuit training in my dressing room..."

"Typical the day I get me scotch eggs out its cloudy!!"

"I reckon I've hit the snooze button about 5 times this morning!! #oops"

"Just strolling around the hotel.. Forgot to look in the mirror when I woke up... realising I have Extreme Bed Head!! Trying to act cool!

"OH MY DAYS!! 4 MILLION twitter followers.. Not sure what to say but just cheers!! Hope I keep things interesting!! Lot of pressure now haha"

"Woke up thinking about pancakes.. Last night I had.. Sugar lemon rolled it, with some ice-cream on top!! #breakfast?!?"

"Doing abit of house cleaning... #messy #whereismymum haha"

Wordsearch

Can you find all of the Olly-related words in our puzzle?

```
R L T F A C F F S M Z X O M O
K L R W N I A S I N J I W F S
B A N Y I C L C T H A B A C A
U B L F T R A N I Y F B H E
S T Y O C O T U R Z R M B L G
Y O R M P U W E Y T R B P P A
S O P H C N C B R O S I V R T
V F O T W I N A R T X U Y O S
O N O I T C E R I D S E A B K
E S I N G I N G R T L K V B M
F L O E A Y C I A N E F R I R
G W Y B Y R D H A P N X P E J
T M Z I J A M T A Y O W U Y S
G Y T W K S S Y K E E H C Z R
N B D Y W T G N U F F T B X D
```

☆ Army   ☆ Factor   ☆ One   ☆ Twin
☆ Australia ☆ Fans   ☆ Rida   ☆ Twitter
☆ Busy   ☆ Football   ☆ Singing   ☆ Xtra
☆ Cheeky   ☆ Hats   ☆ Stage

54

Don't slip up on our tricky wordsearch!

55

Olly

smash hits!

Olly

Body talk

Can you guess which of Olly's body parts we've zoomed in on in our crazy quiz?

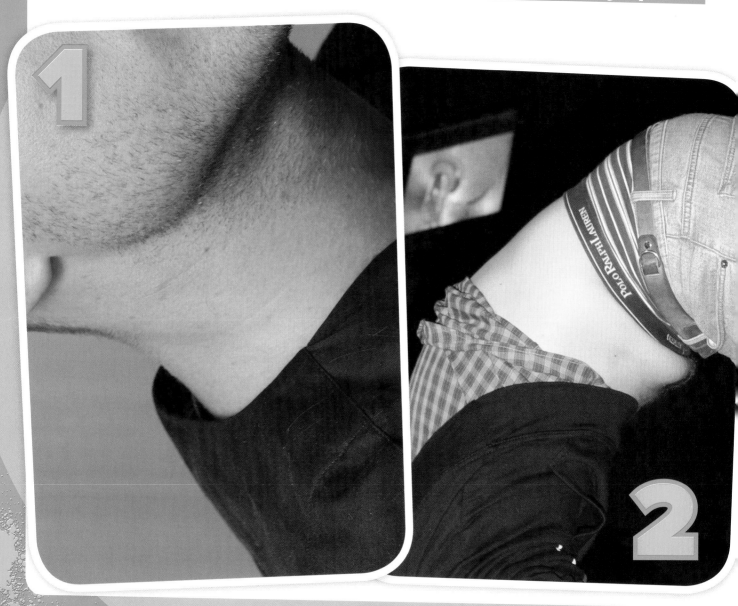

1

2

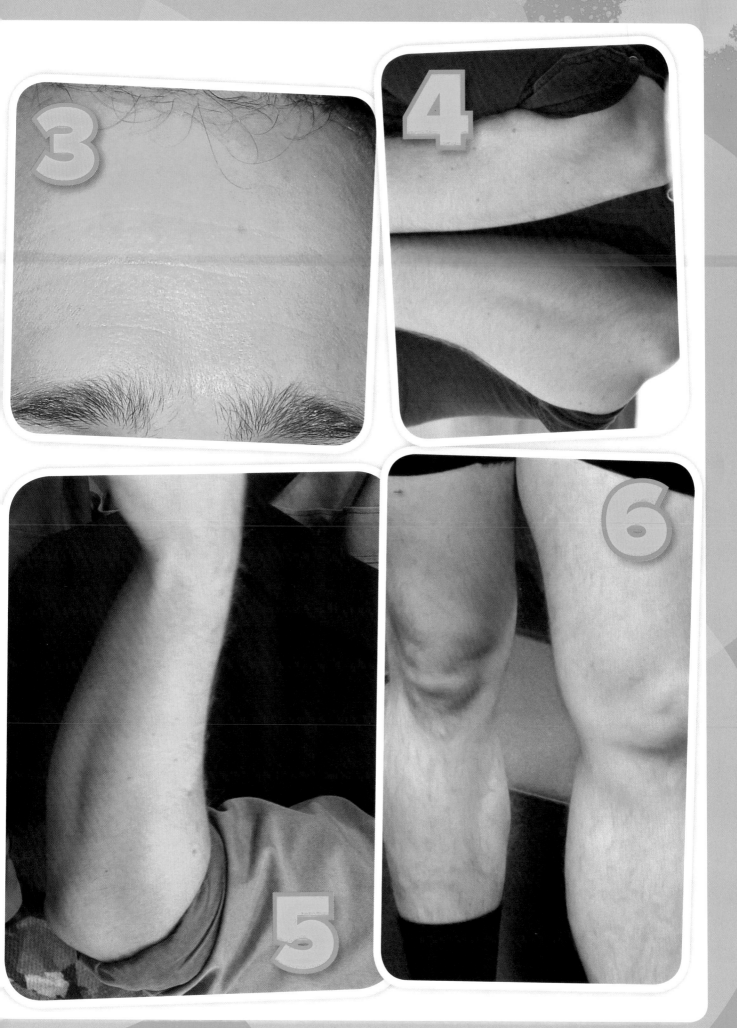

Famous friends

Olly's got his fair share of famous pals.

Check out this cool collection

One Direction

Olly and the lads have been mates for ages and he supported them on tour in America in 2012. He and Niall are such good pals they joke they've got matching chest hair.

Caroline Flack

Caroline and Olly became close thanks to their co-presenting jobs on The Xtra Factor and Caroline has admitted that her mum would love her to marry Ol. Ahhhh!

JLS

The boy bands love Olly! He and the JLS boys have been friends for years. They often play on the same bill at festivals and they've been seen out partying together.

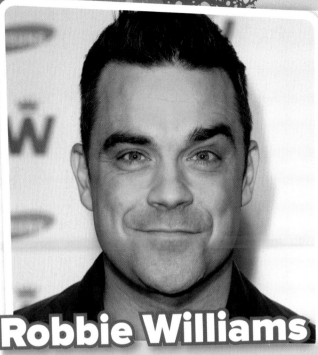

Robbie Williams

Firm friends Olly and Robbie have toured together. Robbie often gives him advice and Olly admits, "He said he sees a lot of me in him – and I see a lot of me in him, too."

Wayne Rooney

Olly and Wayne met when they took part in a tournament for football video game FIFA. Sadly, Olly lost out to the professional player, which doesn't come as much of a surprise!

Loveable Rogues

The Britain's Got Talent trio supported him on tour and they all ended up going clubbing and then partying back at Olly's apartment. Sonny later labeled him 'cool'. He's not wrong!

Olly

Olly

How to pull Olly!

Do you fancy being Mrs Murs? Then follow our tell-all guide to pulling the hot hat-wearing chap

Be yourself

It's one thing being gorge, but if you can't make Murs laugh, it's bye-bye. As he says: "I'm really into personalities. There have been certain girls that I've been attracted to, but when we got to chatting, it was such a let-down. So for me, a great personality is key."

Be a geek!

He's always had a bit of thing for geeky girls. "The geeky girls were always my cup of tea at school. The girls who used to annoy me were the ones who'd say things like, 'What year are you in? Year eight? Sorry, I only go for older guys.'"

Be prepared to be silly!

Olly has a wacky sense of humour, and he's looking for a girl who is just the same. "I just like someone who's up for a laugh and doesn't take herself too seriously. I like girls who want to get up and dance and don't mind singing in front of my family – you know, silly stuff."

Show your fun side

Olly isn't into girls who just want to stand around looking cool. "Some girls won't eat in front of boys or won't go bowling. They just want to go out and look pretty. I don't really get that. I want someone who is up for having a good time."

64

"Come on ladies, I'm still single!"

Impress his parents!

Olly is super-close to his mum and dad Vicky-Lynn and Peter, and any potential gfs will have definitely have to pass the parent test.

"I want to meet a girl who I love and who my parents will like. I want us all to have fun together. That's a massive thing for me."

Don't be impressed by his fame

Olly can see right through ladies who only fancy him because he's famous. "Nine times out of 10 they're really good looking girls that wouldn't even talk to me otherwise, so I just ignore it" he admits.

Definitely don't, ahem, pass wind in front of him

Although he admits he has a few bad habits of his own, he would hate it if a girl was unladylike in his company. "Farting's completely off the radar... If a girl farted in front of me I'd be devastated."

Be ready to settle down

Ol is planning to meet the woman of his dreams pretty soon and says he's already on the lookout for someone to spend his life with.

"I want to be in a stable relationship and have kids by the time I'm 30. I want to be in love and have a wife."

It's written in the stars

Olly is a Taurus, which means that what you see is what you get. People born under the sign of the bull are upfront and honest and you can usually tell what they're thinking just by looking at them. Once they make their minds up about something it's very difficult to change it!

When it comes to relationships they are very loyal. It may take them a while to totally trust someone and commit, but once they do they are one hundred percent supportive and will do everything in their power to keep their other half happy.

Olly may have been single for a while, but that doesn't mean he doesn't have offers. Taureans are very attractive to other people because of their outgoing personalities and cool dress sense

Taureans are romanic and loyal. Hurrah!

(we've all seen those tight trousers and smart shirts), and they like to put other people first.

When Olly does eventually meet his Miss Right he will throw himself into the relationship wholeheartedly, and the lucky lady will be well looked after.

Olly Murs: excited about being Taurus

Taureans like to be romantic and make others feel special, so she can expect lots of candlelit dinners and thoughtful gifts.

When it comes to career, Taurus guys and gals are determined and strong. They have good common sense, which helps when making important business decisions, and they follow their intuition.

On the downside, they can be stubborn (just like a bull!) and they sometimes have a tendency to get a bit lazy if they get the opportunity.

Given the choice between a night out and a night in front of the TV, lazing often wins out because they enjoy their downtime. Sometimes a little bit too much...

All in all they are fun and dependable, but they do like to have their own way! If you want to win Olly's heart show him your light-hearted, laid back side because Taurean's like being with someone they can spend a cosy Saturday night in with. Er, we'll volunteer!

The BIG Quiz

Let's see if you're the quiz Murs-ter...

1 Who is Olly's favourite pop star of all time?

2 What does Olly's nan knit him?

3 What was Olly's first UK number one?

4 What position did Olly come in The X Factor?

5 What is his favourite film?

6 Where did Olly do his trek for Comic Relief?

7 Which brightly coloured sweets does Olly love?

8 Where was Olly born?

9 What is Olly's middle name?

10 What is Olly's star sign?

11 What job was Olly doing before he entered for The X Factor?

12 Which game show has he appeared on twice?

13 What is the name of his debut album?

14 Which one of his singles did Rizzle Kicks feature on?

15 Who is his fave footballer?

16 What's Olly's dad's name?

17 Where is his top holiday destination?

18 What does Olly hold a world record for?

19 Which football team does Olly support?

20 How many BRIT awards has Olbeen nominated for?

Answers on page76

68

Olly

Olly

I love Olly because...

There are probs loads of reasons you heart Olly.

Jot them all down here so you don't forget them!

My favourite Olly single is...

I love it when he wears...

He made me laugh when he...

If I went out on a date with him I would want to go to...

If I could give him any present it would be...

If he bought me a present I would like it to be...

I think Olly is really talented because...

The first time I realised I liked Olly was...

I think Olly and I are most alike because...

If I ever met Olly I would...

Olly is the coolest guy in the world because...

My favourite bit of Olly merchandise I own is...

When I listen to Olly's music it makes me feel...

If I could give Olly one piece of advice it would be...

If Olly came to my house for dinner I would cook him...

Spot the difference

See if you can spot the five funny differences between these two pics of Olly

Answers on page 76

Answers

The Big Quiz

1. Michael Jackson
2. Wooly hats
3. Dance With Me Tonight
4. Second
5. The Goonies
6. Kenya
7. Skittles
8. Essex
9. Stanley
10. Taurus
11. He was a recruitment consultant
12. Deal Or No Deal
13. Olly Murs
14. My Heart Skips A Beat
15. David Beckham
16. Peter
17. Barbados
18. Making the most cups of tea in an hour!
19. Manchester United
20. Four

Wordsearch

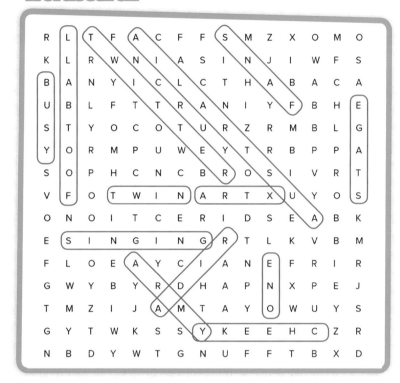

Body talk

1. Chin
2. Torso
3. Forehead
4. Arm
5. Both arms!
6. Legs

Spot the difference

1. Missing microphone
2. "O" missing on the drum
3. Pocket square missing
4. Musician's T-shirt changed colour
5. Flag design changed